BEI GRIN MACHT SICH IHR WISSEN BEZAHLT

AF149915

- Wir veröffentlichen Ihre Hausarbeit,
  Bachelor- und Masterarbeit

- Ihr eigenes eBook und Buch -
  weltweit in allen wichtigen Shops

- Verdienen Sie an jedem Verkauf

Jetzt bei www.GRIN.com hochladen
und kostenlos publizieren

Florian Biehl

Rezension: "Teaching Grammar Creatively"

GRIN Verlag

Bibliografische Information der Deutschen Nationalbibliothek:

Die Deutsche Bibliothek verzeichnet diese Publikation in der Deutschen National-
bibliografie; detaillierte bibliografische Daten sind im Internet über http://dnb.d-
nb.de/ abrufbar.

Impressum:

Copyright © 2010 GRIN Verlag GmbH
Druck und Bindung: Books on Demand GmbH, Norderstedt Germany
ISBN: 978-3-656-58577-0

Dieses Buch bei GRIN:

http://www.grin.com/de/e-book/268310/rezension-teaching-grammar-creatively

GRIN - Your knowledge has value

Der GRIN Verlag publiziert seit 1998 wissenschaftliche Arbeiten von Studenten, Hochschullehrern und anderen Akademikern als eBook und gedrucktes Buch. Die Verlagswebsite www.grin.com ist die ideale Plattform zur Veröffentlichung von Hausarbeiten, Abschlussarbeiten, wissenschaftlichen Aufsätzen, Dissertationen und Fachbüchern.

Besuchen Sie uns im Internet:

http://www.grin.com/

http://www.facebook.com/grincom

http://www.twitter.com/grin_com

Teaching Grammar Creatively

1. Introduction

Teaching Grammar Creatively is a workbook, written by Günter Gernegross et.al., for teachers concerning a new approach to teaching grammar as a second language. After describing their approach, there will be a closer look at the unit dealing with adjectives and adverbs to see how the theory looks like in practice. In the end, there will be a small summary in which there will be shown the positive and negative aspects of this teaching method.

2. Approach

According to the introduction of the book, the aim of the authors is "to stimulate the imagination, humour, and creativity" (Gernegross p.5) of the learners by providing lessons which do not only give pure information but involve the learners in a process of exploration. This will be explained later.

The grammar lessons are divided into two sections, called *Language Awareness Activities* and *Creative Grammar Practice*. Even though these sections are mainly used together, they are self-standing and can be used separately. Should you as a teacher like one part but think of the other one as unfitting for what you intend to do, you can just drop that one and only use the one you feel comfortable with.

Teaching Grammar Creatively works without explicit grammar rules like class-books normally do. The idea behind it is that especially younger learners need to learn more subconsciously. This is called Awareness-raising, meaning the students discover the language and find the rules for themselves while the teacher only provides a frame in which the learners work. This learner-led method is said to be more efficient because these self-done discoveries of rules lead to a reorganisation of the learner's knowledge. Thus the learners have a higher possibility to remember the rules and apply them correctly.

The ability of applying rules subconsciously, rather than knowing them by heart, is the main goal of the whole approach.

3. Language Awareness Activities

The Language Awareness activities or lessons are divided into three sections called *Discovery, Consolidation* and *Use*. This model sounds like the traditional *Presentation, Practice and Production* method which is often used in schools today, but the authors explain the differences between both ideas. (Gernegross p.7 ff)

Because of the learner-led approach, the term *Discovery* is more appropriate than *Presentation* is as the learners are given data or are confronted with problems and then discover the according grammar themselves, instead of learning precisely what a teacher "presents" to them.

According to the author, *Practice* mainly involves the learners in repeating given structures without really realizing how the given structures work. This is where *Consolidation* uses another way. Instead of simply repeating things or having a speaking practice, students will be confronted with understanding tasks. *"For example, students may be asked to read (or listen to) a series of sentences – some including structure X and some including structure Y – and to match these sentences with the appropriate picture."* (Gernegross p.7)

The last section is *Use*. Contrary to *Production*, *Use* means not only that learners produce something concerning the taught grammar, but develop a personalized use. This means students use the new learned item in a context that is important to them. According to the author, language is only memorable when it has been owned.

4. Creative Grammar Practice

Creative Grammar Practice provides further practice of grammar with focus on the individual creativity of the learners. Thus, students are thought to be more motivated.

This section is also divided into a total of four smaller sections: *Lead-in activities, Presentation of model text, Reconstruction of model text* and *Text creation.*

Lead-in activities are meant to be a sort of warm-up for the students and for getting ready to work in a foreign language. *Presentation of model text* is the presentation of a short text which shows the target structure and clarifies its function. In the section *Reconstruction of model text* learners shall remember the model text and recreate it from a gapped version for example. *"[...] By remembering the model text the students can experience a felling of success and gain ability in using structure(s) accurately."* (Gernegross p.9)

Finally, *Text creation* lets students create their own texts within the frame of the model text. This can be done in several ways: groups, orally, written…

5. Theory in practice

After briefly explaining the theory behind *Teaching Grammar Creatively*, there will now be a look on how a chapter of grammar looks like. For this purpose the topic *Adjectives/Adverbs* (Gernegross p.97 ff.) was chosen.

Like most of the units, the topic is subdivided into sections A and B – analogue to *Language Awareness Activity* and *Creative Grammar Practice*. The suggested time of both sections is approximately 50 minutes, thus a little longer than the usual class session.

Section A starts with the aims of the unit, followed by the first sub-section *Discovery*. Herein, the teacher is asked to write the words *good* and *well* on the board. Now, students shall fill the gaps of the sentences *He cooks ___* and *his food smells ___* with the two words. After this, other adjectives and adverbs shall be given that could fill the gaps.

Now, the teacher is adviced to "*highlight the difference between the kind of words that go into the first slot [...] and the kind of words that go into the second slot [...].*" (Gernegross p.97) After this explanation, the learners should complete other gapped sentences.

Now the sub-section *Consolidation* starts. The teacher is advised to write down several adverbs and adjectives and read out a given text that includes gaps again. The learners are supposed to find appropriate adjectives or adverbs for the gap. This could also be done as a kind of competition between groups of learners.

Finally, the sub-section *Use* concludes the first section. The teacher is supposed to write sentence frames on the board: *What makes you feel...? / What makes you react...?* And give a list of words that could complete each frame. After this, learners shall prepare questions to ask one another in pairs or groups and finally report on some of their conversation. This is the end of section A.

Section B starts with advices for the teacher telling him which given texts should be copied. These texts are given on an accompanying CD. The four tasks of text work consist mainly in recreation and gap-filling. Concluding this section, the learners are supposed to go through the texts again and write out adjectives and adverbs. Finally, they shall write their own small texts similar to the ones they worked with. This completes the main-section *Adjectives/Adverbs*.

6. Criticism

In theory, the general attempt of the book to involve the learner's world more into teaching and work less with grammar-rules sounds very good. On a closer look the ideas are not implemented successfully. In this particular case, the students do not discover adjectives and adverbs but are confronted with them and have to differentiate without any hint or clue. The first part is simple guessing and thus becomes a section of trial and failure.

Another problem is that teachers will have to consult other grammar books when they want explicit information about a certain topic. *"Highlight the difference between the kind of words that go into the first slot [...] and the kind of words that go into the second slot [...]."* (Gernegross p.97) is not a very helpful comment.

There may also be a problem with the selection of the words with which the author starts here. By using irregular adjectives and adverbs (good, well), learners might get confused and are not able to apply or find a useful rule on which is used when.

In section B are other problems. Although the author speaks against simply repeating what the teacher says, gap-filling and text reconstruction is nothing but repeating given structures. The very good and important aspect of involving the grammar into the situation of the learners is only done right in the end with only one task. This promising concept should have been used more often throughout the section.

A minor problem is the suggested time of the section, which lies by approximately 50 minutes, thus is longer than a class session.

In conclusion it can be said that the main principle behind this approach in grammar teaching seems very promising, but has minor problems which should be manageable by the teachers using the book. On the other hand, teachers are supported with a big amount of texts and hand-outs which can easily be adjusted to their own principles of teaching.

Bibliography

Gerngross, Günter, et.al. 2006 Teaching Grammar Creatively CUP